Made in United States
Orlando, FL
25 July 2022

20156324R00061